Modern Artists

Jenkins

Harry N. Abrams, Inc., Publishers, New York

Jean Cassou

Jenkins

Standard Book Number: 8109–4404–9
Library of Congress Catalogue Card Number: 64–17174

Cassou   Until now I had the impression that your painting was interesting above all for its energy and dynamic quality; to me, it was a painting of instinct, like the majority of modern American painting which, to put it simply, stems from Pollock and is a painting of *élan*, of dynamic character, manifesting a great gestural, muscular and vital power. In short, a painting which is somewhat biological and certainly very interesting. Take Pollock, he was a very great artist, of a truly inspired nature, and he gave a tremendous stimulus to all modern painting. And so I had the impression, Paul Jenkins, that you were linked to this movement and that you situated yourself in the continuation of this form of creation.

On seeing your painting in your studio and on examining it at close range, I realize that it is something completely different, that, on the contrary, it is much more deliberate and more guided than my first impression led me to believe. Obviously there is that *élan vital*, the organic impulse that is so characteristic of your country and situates you in the present-day American school, but there is also a great deal of 'art', and there is *painting*. There is a great love of painting, carefully executed, thought out, directed and guided. First of all, I see a touching concern for textural quality. There is an affinity between your temperament and the material used. These extraordinary blacks, worked, very sustained, and of a wonderful density with a grain and a substance, are not only the vehicle of a movement, or the expression of a gesture, but are the result of worked painting, elaborated and set on the canvas in certain places and producing forms. And then, this black is modulated: it is not simply thrown on the canvas, but worked. Finally, there are elements of colour which play their rôle in all the painting, especially these outstanding blues. Then, when we see the large black forms tossed across the white surface, we notice that there is something underneath, that there are intentions, an entire intellectual and technical elaboration, and that all this is by no means pure chance and pure instinct. No, I recognize here what we should call 'art'.

I should like to question you on precisely the characteristics of this art. I was struck by the fact that the titles of all these paintings are preceded by the term 'Phenomena' and I should like to ask you what you mean by this. Is every canvas a phenomenon, that is to say, a manifestation of something, a reality? Or is it a generic name that covers a certain number of canvases? I should like to know, in fact, what you mean by this notion of phenomenon.

Jenkins	Phenomenon, for me, is involved with the capture of the ever-changing reality, both in the act of painting and the final result. I am drawn to the ever-changing realities not because they seem to be the expression of a hazardous world, but because they draw me closer to the wonders. This incites me not just to accept change but to *induce* it. A phenomenon which springs from the course of events, which happens, is something we adjust to and always have to investigate anew.
Cassou	If I have understood correctly, this phenomenon is a manifestation, an event. Yes, I have the impression that this could be translated by 'event'. Something happens, there is an occasion for something to occur. Originally this something is subjective in character and becomes objective on the canvas. The result then is a manifestation. Something manifests itself. Something happens. Therefore a deep intimacy exists between the state of the creator's mind and the act of painting; the latter is a direct manifestation, a direct expression of this subjective phenomenon, this spiritual event, this thing which he feels, and of his need to manifest and produce himself. In your idea I see the union of two poles of creation, of two elements of creation. On the one hand, an inner necessity and on the other, a work of art. A work of art which is achieved and which in itself has as much importance as what you feel, because to the initial impulse are added consciousness, technical control and will.
Jenkins	The conscious intention occurs in the act of painting. 'The-thing-as-it-changes' is captured. There is something inscrutable about the familiar, something unknown, and this unknown is what I try to discover by approaching it indirectly.
Cassou	The *métier* I admired in these paintings, which struck me and was the revelation I had on seeing the paintings in your studio, this *métier*, as I call it, is not just a result of knowledge and understanding, a creative or plastic experience, separated from inspiration and from the creative operation itself. It is not something which you possess in the sense in which people say, 'This painter is very accomplished' or, 'This painter knows his craft'. On the contrary, it is some-

6

thing which is created in every one of your paintings and is enriched from painting to painting. But it will never constitute a theoretical doctrine, practical knowledge, or a formula.

Here, quite the contrary, the *métier* is created by each painting and is revealed, strengthened, fortified and increased each time.

Jenkins   Sometimes it seems as though I am keeping a storm door shut with one hand while I am painting with the other, in order to keep the known out so that the unknown may enter. To lean too heavily on *métier* could mean the end of discovery. On the other hand, to trust entirely to inspiration could lead to a hermetic art enclosed only in the arms of one beholder. I avoid considering the two separately, and work towards bringing them together.

Cassou   Before the diversity and instantaneousness of the creative artist's experiences, we again find ourselves brought back to emphasizing its inner forces, its subjectivity. Nevertheless, I continue to feel preoccupied by the question of the relationship between this extremely strong and powerful subjectivity which at each new sensation absolutely must express itself, and, on the other hand, the constraints of the *métier* and of the art and technique which seems to me to have great importance in your work. This entire art has sensitivity, represents knowledge and understanding and research. And so I wonder how all this is reconciled and how the primary impulse, so strong, so violent and always so new, adapts itself to purely technical problems and necessities. Do you not sometimes feel constrained by the materials you use, the size of the canvas you paint?

Jenkins   The very size of the canvas dictates to me. A blank canvas does not frighten me. Even the grain of the canvas gives me a clue. I once did a series of paintings, called the 'Eyes of the Dove', all of a standard size – 30 by 40 inches. There I discovered that one painting might seem to contract and concentrate, fold into itself, but another might appear to expand beyond its boundaries. All achieved a difference of scale. My eye measured a reality which had nothing to do with the arbitrary scale of a yardstick.

Cassou   Here we find the eternal problems of poetic and artistic creation. There is an original, primordial, personal impulse to create something, to express oneself, to manifest oneself. Then, there are the necessities of the *métier*, there is art itself. The value of an artist will be the more significant the more his art is rich, skilful and original, and expressive of his subjective intentions. At this moment we are in fact discussing the fundamental problem of creation as it has always presented itself since painters have existed and have painted. It is a good thing that each artist should communicate his way of being aware of the problems which inevitably become his own problems. What is interesting is for the general problem of art to become a special problem of this or that artist. Moreover, there would be no painting if there were no painters, if, since time began, there were not an infinite number of personal problems, personal ways of treating the same essential and eternal problem. I shall therefore continue to question you on this personal way you have of seeing a problem, which I am presenting in its general and eternal aspects. I quite understand, and you have indicated, the way in which at the moment of the creative act there is reconciled in you your subjective impulse and the necessities of the *métier* which in the very act of creation become your own *métier* and your own, rich and subtle art. I am now going to try and find another point whereby this basic necessity is reconciled with other elements, with other terms and treatments. This time no longer with the *métier*, but at the very origin, with nature and outer reality. You are an abstract painter, but I find in your painting certain relationships with reality. In fact, when we put ourselves in that innermost part of yourself, we see that there is above all a very great force, a primordial energy, but finally this energy is going to be combined with other elements. It is combined with nature, with reality. Your inner force, of which you are aware in your very vocation as a painter and in the instinct which forces you to produce a painting, this 'Phenomenon' which is a painting, well, this harmonises with the natural forces. You sense them – the proof is that you give your paintings titles and that these titles evoke things of reality, things which are especially alive and especially strong. There is a very beautiful painting by you entitled 'Phenomena White Whale'.

Briefly, your titles have a poetic, natural character which is especially striking and I should like you to tell me how you yourself are aware of your relationships with nature to the point of feeling yourself drawn to giving such titles to your paintings.

La Fenêtre

Water Crane

Jenkins   Knowing one cannot know all there is to know, see all there is to see, we must perceive what we can. I do not suffer the illusion that we can see life like a form which we can walk around and see on all four sides. In my paintings I try to indicate with a title an aspect of the work which will leave one free to dwell on it without having to look for the subject. The title I decide on is one that leaves the painting free to be itself and not about something.

The 'White Whale' still leaves us space in the mind to wonder. We are not concerned about its being just a fish, or a symbol, or some kind of threat to our sense of the unknown. The 'White Whale' is an enigma not just the haunting, tormenting challenge for Ahab.

And we know something else about nature which has changed not just our attitude towards it but our very lives. It is still hard for us to believe that sunlight and candlelight were what we read by or saw the enemy by. That kind of light accustomed the eye to see reality in terms of sculptural dimension. We perceive and see differently. Our light world is caught in refraction and interpenetration of light. Streets become halls of mirrors, temperature zones contrast violently. We do not see all there is to see but what we can see. The adventure being to distinguish the real universe of ourselves from the other one we reel through. Nature has most meaning for me when, through a state of being, rather than watching, I am able to find meanings, visual meanings.

Cassou   This is a very rewarding self-analysis. Nevertheless, I should like to stress my question with all its elementary character: How do you feel your relationship with the outer world, not only as it is perceived by our senses, but also as it is imagined and felt? How do you conceive the influence or the existence of this understanding of the outer world within your creative experience? What is the relationship between the understanding you have of the outer world, this relationship you feel in yourself with the outer world, and, on the other hand, your creative experience?

Jenkins   Let us take a reality which is forever before us and unchanging. In name, it remains the same as it was for Masaccio, as it was for Cézanne, as it was for Monet. Let us take the apparent reality that is the colour *green*. It has been here as long as we know. So green becomes a challenge. To transform this colour into an individual part of oneself, it is

13

essential to make a rediscovery of the colour, to give it a special and particular meaning that was not there before and does not necessarily have to be optical or in the mind's eye, or a remembered dream; it can be a sensation that becomes a compulsion.

When you look at that green, you know where it comes from; it comes from nature, but nature in the sense that you resist nature. *Green* becomes your own experience within it, and in turn it becomes an entity in itself. This is what Mondrian achieved when he took a colour and made it exist within its own right, giving it no reference other than its own; and yet how well we know that he knew about trees. Nature is something you come to resist but one cannot get away from it.

Cassou I think that the act of giving a title to a painting is something extremely important and can greatly enlighten us on the conception that each painter has of his own aesthetics. Therefore, you give your paintings titles and naturally, as usually happens in the form of art you are practising, you give these titles after having finished the painting. Well, when you give a title to a painting which you have just finished or, sometimes, which you made several days previously, do you have the impression that this invention of a title is a new act? Is it a concept born from the painting you are considering and which awakens in you an idea, and is it this idea that will give you a title for your painting? Or, do you recognize in this title certain states preliminary to your creative act, certain sensations you could have had at the origin of the painting you made, a perception you would have had, a feeling you would have felt and which would have let loose in you the gesture which achieved the painting? Is the title something utterly new in you and a second creation born of the consideration of your painting, of your encounter with your painting? Or else, do you recognize in this title an element of your primordial and original inspiration?

Jenkins Titles for me are like names on a map of the artist's world. I try to find the identity word that will secure an attitude towards the painting rather than provoke a visual object that the eye will seek out.

I like 'Phenomena Yellow Will Out' because it sounds like an irrational statement of fact, or 'Phenomena Lifted 14

Stigma' which is free of a previous association of what it should look like. Sometimes a contradictory title like 'Phenomena Heaven Crawl' will still establish an identity.

The artist has within his world a galaxy of thoughts and images which return to him ever new born. Even in the most changing world of phenomena reoccurrence is experienced. Rediscovery of the haunting image is not an experience of repetition. Each time it is experienced differently, yet has to be consistent with that specific world the artist creates and is committed to.

Cassou   You give the impression of being an American artist with all the virtues, all the characteristics which we associate with American artists, that is to say, great simplicity, great vital force, very young and very fresh, a kind of ingenuousness in the face of life, the world and art, which is something extremely comforting in our time. I think that it is here that present-day American art contributes something to universal painting. And then, at the same time, within this very generality, you have your personality which is original and which even exceeds the limits of this definition. What is interesting in you is precisely this reconciliation of a very great creative force, a very great plastic force, and a poetic world; this reconciliation, the intimate relationship between these two domains, this, it seems to me, is what makes you a complete artist.

Lotus

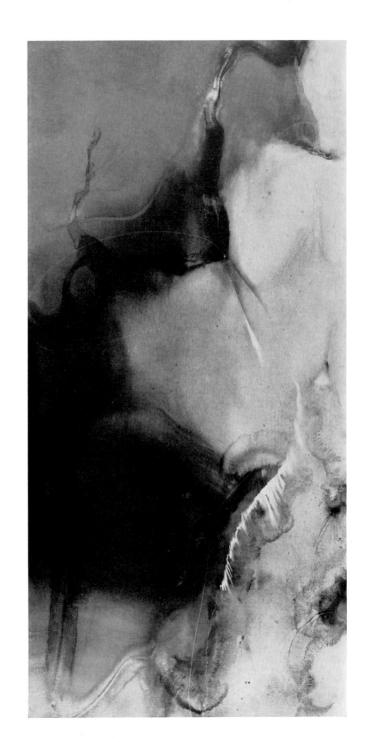

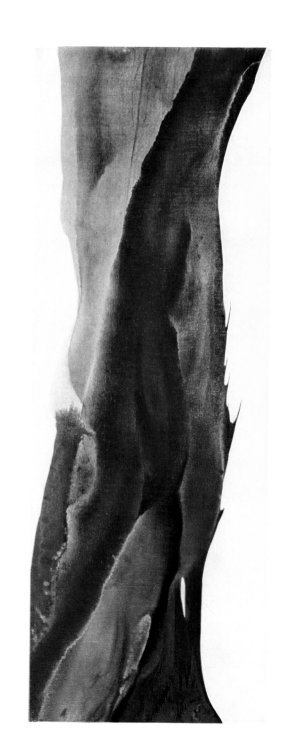

Phenomena Falling Mountain

Phenomena Missing Trinity

Phenomena–Big Blue

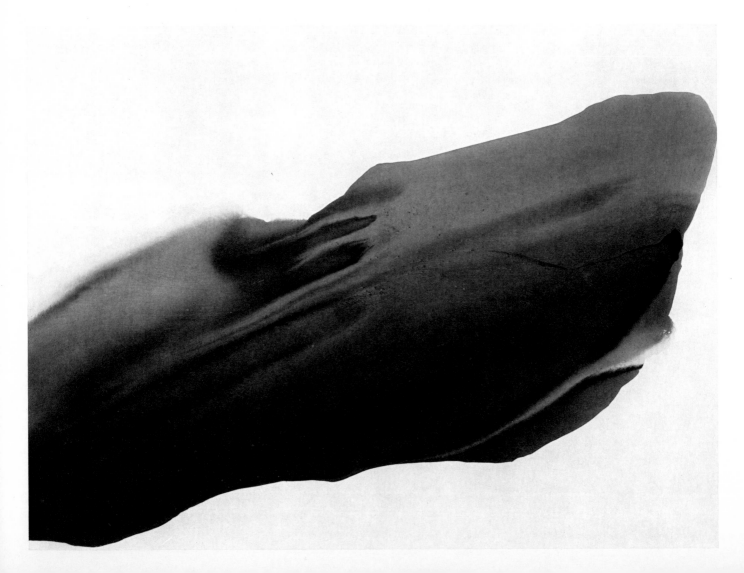

Phenomena Ring Rang Rung

Phenomena Over Cowl

Phenomena Aftermath

46

Phenomena Votive

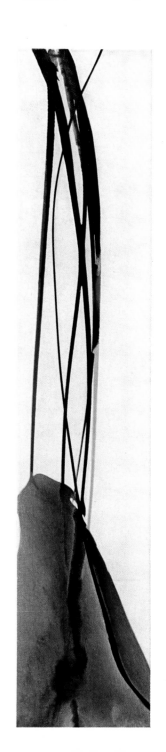

53   Phenomena With Devil's Cap

Phenomena Blue Loop

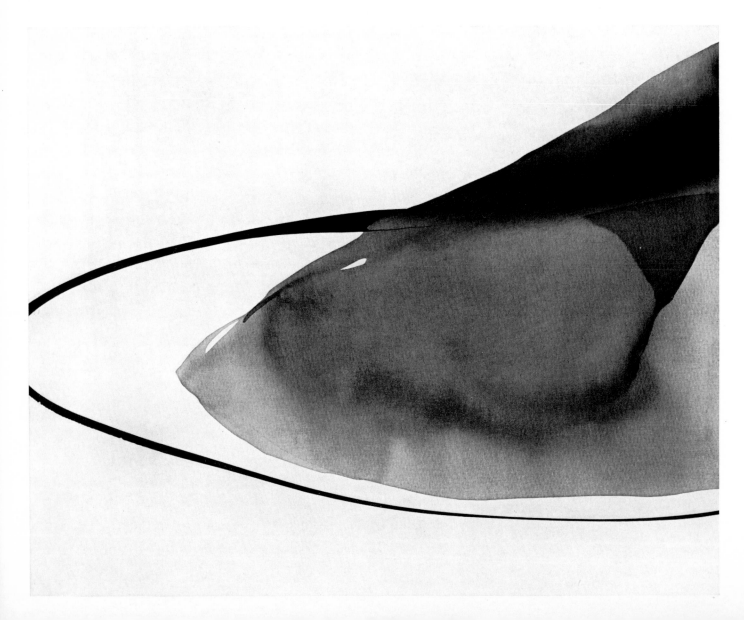

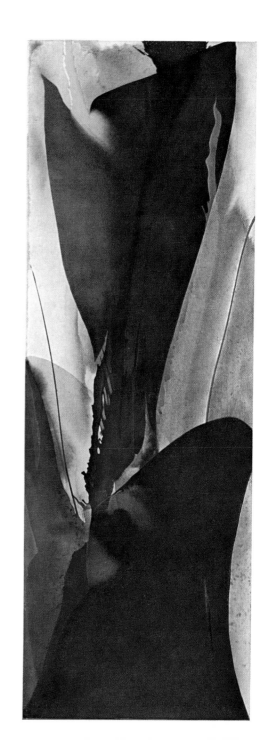

57   Phenomena Marauder

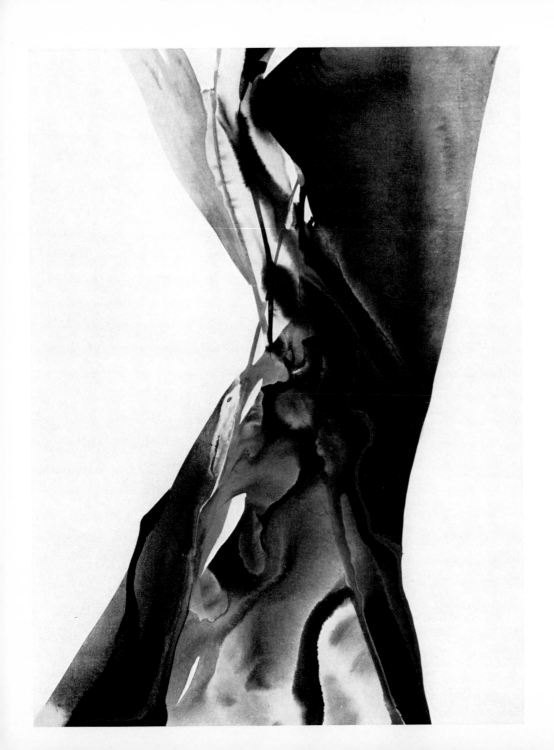

List of Plates

33 Phenomena Tide Finder, 1961. Oil on canvas, 97 ×195 cm.
Martha Jackson Gallery, New York

35 Phenomena Ramashandra Ramashandra, 1962. Oil on canvas, 195 ×150 cm.
Coll. Robert Shoenberg, Saint Louis, Miss.

36 Phenomena Brimstone, 1961. Oil on canvas, 177 ×130 cm.
Coll. Hermann Igell, Stockholm

37 Phenomena Over Cowl, 1961. Oil on canvas, 61 ×50 cm.
Coll. Dr Kaishi Ohashi, Tokyo

39 Phenomena Wakiyashi, 1961. Oil on canvas, 100 ×65 cm.
Musée National d'Art Moderne, Paris

40 Phenomena Wing Off, 1961. Oil on canvas, 130 ×162 cm.
Coll. William Rubin, New York

41 Phenomena Heaven Under, 1961. Oil on canvas, 130 ×130 cm.
Coll. Baroness Alix de Rothschild, Paris

43 Phenomena Red Wing, 1962. Oil on canvas, 100 ×100 cm.
Coll. David Kluger, New York

44 Phenomena Imperial Range, 1962. Oil on canvas, 114 ×146 cm.
Coll. Mrs Albert D. Lasker, New York

45 Phenomena The Place Of Quarterstaff, Paris 1962. Oil on canvas, 195 ×97 cm.
Gallery Tooth & Sons, Ltd., London

46 Phenomena Aftermath, 1962. Oil on canvas, 153 ×294 cm.
Bezalel Museum, Jerusalem

47 Phenomena To Troll, Paris 1962. Oil on canvas, 130 ×89 cm.
Galerie Karl Flinker, Paris

49 Phenomena Play Of Trance, Paris 1962. Oil on canvas, 162 ×130 cm.
Coll. Karl Flinker, Paris

50 Phenomena Blue Carries, 1962. Oil on canvas, 174 ×114 cm.
Solomon R. Guggenheim Museum, New York

51 Phenomena Votive, Paris 1962/63. Oil on canvas, 195 ×150 cm.
The Walker Art Gallery, Liverpool

53   Phenomena With Devil's Cap, Paris 1963. Oil on canvas, 120×25 cm.
Coll. Nancy Balfour, London

54   Phenomena Blue Loop, Paris 1963. Oil on canvas, 65×81 cm.
Coll. Basil de Ferranti, London

55   Phenomena Indigo Span, Paris 1963. Oil on canvas, 170×120 cm.
Gavin Cochrane, London

57   Phenomena Marauder, Paris 1962/63. Oil on canvas, 195×68 cm.
Coll. of the artist

58   Phenomena For Salomé, 1963. Oil on canvas, 116×89 cm.
Coll. Ernesto Wolf, São Paulo

59   Phenomena With Ides, 1963. Oil on canvas, 116×89 cm.
Galerie Karl Flinker, Paris

61   Phenomena Nearing Isthmus, Paris 1962/63. Oil on canvas, 120×170 cm.
Coll. C. C. Martin, Los Angeles

1923	Born in Kansas City, Missouri
1938–41	Kansas City Art Institute and apprentice in a ceramic factory
1948–51	Art Students' League, New York
1953	Came to Paris. From that time he has been living and working both in Paris and New York
1954	First one-man show in Paris, Studio Paul Facchetti. One-man show, Zimmergalerie Franck, Frankfurt/Main
1955	One-man show, Zoe Dusanne Gallery, Seattle, Wash. Artistes Etrangers en France, Petit Palais, Paris
1956	Galerie Rive Droite and Galerie Stadler, Paris. First New York one-man show, Martha Jackson Gallery. Co-editor of 'Observations of Michel Tapié', Wittenborn Publications Forecast, American Federation of Arts. Recent Drawings USA, Museum of Modern Art, New York. New Trends in Paintings, Arts Council of Great Britain, London
1957	The Exploration of Paint with Dubuffet, Francis and Riopelle, Arthur Tooth & Sons, London. One-man show, Galerie Stadler, Paris. Young America 1957, Whitney Museum of American Art, New York. Orto Arte, Sala Gaspar, Barcelona and Madrid
1958	Carnegie International, Pittsburgh. Nature Abstracted, Whitney Museum of American Art, New York. Biennial exhibition, Corcoran Gallery, Washington D. C. One-man show, Martha Jackson Gallery, New York
1959	One-man show, Galerie Stadler, Paris. Kunstverein, Cologne. Turin Art Festival, Turin. Gutai Festival, Osaka, Japan
1960	One-man show, Arthur Tooth & Sons, London. One-man show, Martha Jackson Gallery, New York. Galerie Karl Flinker, Paris
1961	One-man show, Galerie Karl Flinker, Paris. One-man show, Martha Jackson Gallery, New York. Carnegie International, Pittsburgh. U.S.I.S. American Artists, London. Publication of 'Paul Jenkins' by James Fitzsimmons, Kenneth B. Sawyer and Pierre Restany (Ed. Two Cities, Paris). Abstract Expressionists & Imagists, Solomon R. Guggenheim Museum, New York

1962   Watercolour-show, Galerie Karl Flinker, Paris. One-man show, Esther Robles Gallery, Los Angeles. One-man show, Galleria Toninelli, Milan. Salon de Mai, Paris. Gegenwart 62, Haus am Waldsee, Berlin. Whitney Annual, New York. One-man show, Galerie Charles Lienhard, Zürich. One-man show, Galleria Odyssia, Rome. One-man show, Kunstverein, Cologne. Ecole de Paris, Galerie Charpentier, Paris. Seattle World's Fair, Seattle, Wash.

1963   Art: USA: Now: Royal Academy, London, Tokyo, etc. One-man show, Arthur Tooth & Sons, London. One-man show, Galerie Karl Flinker, Paris. Galerie Eva de Burén, Stockholm. Réalités Nouvelles, Musée d'Art Moderne, Paris. American Artists A–Z, Art Institute Chicago and American Cultural Center, Paris

1964   One-man show, Kestner-Gesellschaft, Hanover. One-man show, Martha Jackson Gallery, New York. One-man show, Tokyo Gallery, Tokyo. Painting and Sculpture of a Decade, Tate Gallery, London